Aïsha Abdelfatah is a philosophy student in Belgium. Having struggled with her mental health for years, reading and writing have offered a way to cope with the often harsh reality of life. Her search for an understanding and acceptance of this reality has had a large impact on her writing and the topics she explores there.

To Inge for sticking with me through the good and the bad.

To Jorrit and Tessa for encouraging me and bearing with me through this process.

To my brother for motivating me to pursue my passions.

To my mother for believing in me, even when I gave her every reason not to.

I couldn't have done this without you, I love you all.

Aïsha Abdelfatah

DIONYSIAN PESSIMIST

AUSTIN MACAULEY PUBLISHERS™
LONDON • CAMBRIDGE • NEW YORK • SHARJAH

A CIP catalogue record for this title is available from the British Library.

ISBN 9781035853311 (Paperback)
ISBN 9781035853328 (ePub e-book)

www.austinmacauley.com

First Published 2024
Austin Macauley Publishers Ltd®
1 Canada Square
Canary Wharf
London
E14 5AA

I would like to thank Austin Macauley Publishers for giving me this opportunity and for bringing this work to life.

The process of writing this collection has often proved itself to be painful and exhausting and has left me doubting myself and my capabilities. I would not have been able to write it without my friends who have helped me through the self-doubt and anxiety, and my mother for always insisting I could do whatever I set my mind to. They are the reason this book exists and I am beyond grateful. Without them, without their support and their love, this dream of mine, which to me has always felt more like folly than fate, would never have come to be.

We got along like a house on fire
I guess I've always been good
At burning things to the ground
I treat my lovers like enemies looking to plunder
Scorch the earth running from my feelings
They say ash makes for more fertile ground
But it's been a while
Since I've let anything grow

I breathed him in
The way I would breathe air
After a deep dive in the ocean
Deeply
Greedily
Quickly
And soon found out
That even though our lungs love oxygen
It will eventually leave them burnt

We fit together so perfectly
You've never seen something burn as brightly
As his flames
Lighting up my structure

You
Unreachable sun
And I
Your faithful moon
Always trying to catch the barest glimpse
Of your blinding light
But never close enough to feel
Your scorching heat

You
False God
My beautiful lie
More plague than paradise
You told me faith
Is proven through suffering and sacrifice
My body both cross and crucified

You
Godly and graceful
A statue I kneel before
My bruised knees feel holy
When I worship at your alter
But my hopeless prayers
Still remain unanswered
This forbidden fruit tastes so sweet
Because it's already rotten

Like grapes on a vine
He popped parts of me into his mouth
One by one
Savouring every bite
Until there was nothing left of me to swallow

He squeezes my heart in his fist
Needing to see me drip from his fingertips
Not knowing I already ache and bleed for him

You
With your black hole heart
You swallowed me whole
Licked your fingers clean
And decided I wasn't enough
To sate your hunger

I am the waxing moon
I draw him to me like the tides
It is in his ocean
That I baptise myself
Meaning
I will drown myself in his holy water
And he will leave me
Waning
Weeping

Trust me

He whispered

I love you

And I watched as he pulled me apart like forbidden fruit

Hungry

But once he found my bruised core

He just threw me aside

Stay

I cried

But he did not turn around

Come back

I begged

But no God would hear my prayers

If only he'd known that bruised fruit tastes the sweetest

Inside
This gaping wound
This cavernous hollow
As if God himself reached down from heaven
Scraped every last bleeding bit of you out of my chest
And said trust me, this is for the best

What a horrid affliction it is
To be a hopeless romantic
In a world
Where apathy and detachment
Have become the norm

What a cruel fate it is
To have a heart
Brimming with sweet intoxication
When you're left
To drink its bittersweet wine
Alone

I want an astronaut to find me
I want him to look at the galaxies within me
And not shy away
I want him to remember the stars
No matter how vast and dark my universe may be

I want a deep-sea diver to find me
I want him to look at the deep dark depths of me
And not be afraid to swim
I want him to look at my polluted waters
And see something worth saving

I want an archaeologist to find me
I want him to look at my collapsed structure
And realize the kind of storms I must have lived through
I want him to look at my ruins and whisper
Beautiful
Because even though I have buckled under the weight
Of everything life has thrown at me
Part of me is still standing

People seem to think my heart
Is a pavement
Have walked all over it so many times
That it beats to the rhythm of their footsteps

I hope that
In time
The cracks in my concrete will be more
Than something for people to trip over
I hope the soil underneath remembers its own existence
I hope it remembers how to grow

Kneeling
You let parts of me
Dissolve on the tongue
With eyes closed in ecstasy
And let your greedy lips
Linger on my skin
Already hungry
For another taste
Because to worship means to devour
And you have savoured every bite

We tear each other apart
With the softest touch
I guess we're all cannibals at heart

They say God created us in his image
And you recreated God in mine
Blasphemed your way
Into a new religion
And made me die for your sins

You made his voice fit
Behind my milk and honey lips
And in the way of church and men
You put words in my mouth
Made me speak of laws
You had no intention of abiding
And in the way of sinners
You committed your crimes
Only to beg my forgiveness
When the deed was done

The milk and honey on your lips
Made your kiss feel like holy communion
My love you tasted so sweet
With your skin between my teeth

After years of swallowing her words
Is it any wonder a woman
Would tear a lover to shreds
And gorge herself on the poetry of his flesh
That after years of biting her tongue
She would sink her teeth into something that nourishes
That she would let him drip down her chin
Licking him off her fingertips
And whisper thanks for his grace
As he feeds her

My love has always been a weapon
But when I hold its blade against his throat
He does not pull away
He leans into the edge of it
Blood trickling down
And tells me how he loves the sting of me

I think I may have lost my heart
I think it may have crawled its way out of my chest
When you kissed my forehead
Decided it wanted to stay
So it hid under your bed
And lies there collecting dust
I have tried to coax it out
Because the phantom pains get hard to handle
But I guess it's yours now
I guess I will learn to live without it

I think of love like an insatiable hunger
Like black holes swallowing suns
Their darkness all consuming and oppressive
Devouring everything in their path
Letting nothing escape or survive

I tell him I feel empty
I tell him I like it that way
And he asks if I wouldn't rather have happy
No
I say
Because happy feels so much like sad
Happy feels like my father
Telling me that I am not depressed
That I am doing this for attention
Feelings
I tell him
Are like girls in bathrooms
They always bring a friend
Happy and sad share their best friend guilty
But empty braves the trip alone
I tell him that I often feel lonely
And that lonely feels deserved
He asks me why
He tells me I am not ugly
And I laugh
I tell him that ugly is not what scares them away
I tell him that it's hard for people to love the depthless dark
When they have always slept with the lights on
I tell him that people don't like braving this haunted house
Where my ghosts roam free
I tell him that lonely feels

deserved
Because people don't have
the time to wait for their
glue
To dry between
my countless cracks
So they go before it's set
And leave my structure to collapse
I tell him that lonely feels
deserved
Because I don't want people to have
to pour their happy
Into my glass half empty
To fill it to the brim
What I don't tell him is
Even though I feel that way
I still wake up in the middle of the night
And feel this phantom pain
Of a missing body
That I buy dresses for dates
And anniversaries
Even though I know the only anniversary I have to celebrate
Is that of my depression
I don't remember exactly when we first met
But we've been together for a while now
Sometimes it feels like
Depression is a man
And God
Disappointed in his creation
Turned me back into one of his ribs

Actaeon

He comes upon me
Wild and wicked
All edge and point
The only softness to be found
Is the flesh he wants to tear into
But I am not soft
I am the wilderness
The wickedness
I take hold of all who enter
So he comes upon me
Scratched and bleeding
Having tangled with the thorns of me
Yet I will not let him leave
So I take the hunter
I turn him into prey
And watch
As he is torn apart

My love swallowed me whole
Left me buried in the graveyard of his feelings
And didn't give me a second thought
My love had a heart like a broken cross
The edges of it begging for sacrifice
But I refused to be his martyr
Refused to die for someone else's sin
So I clawed my way out of his chest
Out of his throat
I came out the same way his voice did
Whenever he spoke of love
Sharp
Shaking
Trembling
He made I love you sound like the stutter of a shotgun
So violent in its uncertainty, so certain in its violence
Made it sound like a question I never knew the answer to
Like a vow, I would inevitably break

He sweeps to his knees before me
Holds my name on his tongue like a prayer
And lets himself get caught up in my holy rapture

He falls for me
Knees bruised and bloody
Singing psalms while palms sting
Scraped from the stumble into my holy land
So I feed him my milk and honey
Give him my blood and body
And let him eat his fill

But I am a jealous God
And his worship is hard-won and difficult to come by
He sates his thirst and hunger
But mine is not his only altar
My blessings not enough

I am a vengeful God
So when he can fall to his knees
But cannot fall in love
I will let him fall
The same way Lucifer fell
Full of pride and out of grace
And then he will learn
That I am not the forgiving kind

My heart is an open book
By which I mean
You stumbled upon my pages
And wrote yourself into the margins
I had never felt so full
My spine bent
Straining under the weight of your multitudes
You
You dogeared me
Whenever I whispered your name
It was muscle memory to spread myself open
To your favourite part
I thought
I thought
I thought
I could have been your favourite book
The one you always return to
Turn to when you need comforting
I thought
I could have been an easy answer
To the questions, you didn't even know your heart was
asking
But you
You thought I was just easy
A guilty pleasure
Something you hide under the sheets

So no one sees
What you do to take the edge off
I should have known better
Than to think outside my genre
My storyline
My character arc

My heart is an open book
By which I mean
You dropped it on your bedroom floor
Never giving it a second thought

I want I want I want
I am Tantalus
Plagued by my desires
My torment never-ending
Always thirsting and hungering
For something just out of reach
For love
And beauty
And admiration
And so my life remains unlived
For I can never satisfy my hunger
My thirst will never be quenched
I have made my dreams into a nightmare
My wishes have turned my life to dust

The man
He lures me with a siren song
Beckons me with his tales
But the tales he tells are mine
I am caught on his lips like a hook
His every word the bait I cling onto
And he sings to me
Songs of my odyssey
And leaves me to drown in my own longing

He was heavenly
Starry-eyed and beautiful
Dark and all-consuming
Divine like the gods of old
Splendid but fickle
Breathtaking and cruel
It is a terrible burden to love a god
It is a heavy load
To hold up the heavens
As a show of faith
Yet still I remain his Atlas
And strain under the weight of it

Syrinx and Pan

I ran like the wind
Gasping for breath
Feet bleeding and arms scratched
He does not understand
That I do not want to be chased
He hunts me
Like a wolf who's smelled blood
He follows the trail I leave
Lusting after the flesh he will sink his teeth into
I beg I cry I pray
And the gods
They listen
I am wind I am earth I am water flowing
I am the reeds by the river
Gently swaying in the breeze
But still

I do not escape his torment
He cuts me down
And plays me like an instrument
I cannot speak
But my weeping is music to his ears
When he pours into me
I never wished to take his breath away

Pain takes on many forms
Some days it's clenched fists
Nails digging crescent moons into the surface
Until it's the only place that aches

It's hands pulling hair
Clawing skin
Beating until bleeding
Wishing they were used for tenderness instead

And sometimes
It's a heart
Clenching
Pulling in on itself
Foetal position
Wishing it had been spared
The cruelty of love

My love
My soul
My Promethean punishment
Eating away at me
The curse of enlightenment
A gift I never wanted
Its heavenly fire leaving me scorched
So I sit
At the bank of the river Lethe
And drown my fever in it
I fill up my cup
Tasting the sweet forgetfulness
And so in ignorant bliss
I am devoured

An ode to Eibhlín Dubh

I kneel down beside him
Knees and palms slipping
His soul staining clothes
It flows like a river
And my palms turn cups
Swallowing him by the mouthful
This fountain of youth
Can only be brought forth in death
When flowers have bloomed
From decaying flesh
Nonetheless
I will drink
And my tears will become the river
I will eat
And turn myself to stone

They break my body like bread
Get drunk on my blood like wine
Clinking glasses
overflowing
The sweet intoxication of it
flowing from me
I have never owned this
body
Turn me to cross
Crucify me
Make me martyr of their
sins
Imagine me
Unwilling saint
My baptism of pain
My blood leaves their
hands stained
Red
Red
Red
Dripping
The devotees
Gorging themselves on my
holy
Imagine me
Sinful thought

Vilified for their greed
As they take what they
want from me
I have never owned this
body
Imagine me
Looted temple
They enter me without
knocking
Worship at unwilling altar
Demand what I did not
offer
And take what they please
They break this body like
bread
And when they have eaten
their fill
They leave me
Scraping together the
crumbs of it

When I came to the end of
me
I found a creature there
Crouched down on the
ground
All teeth and claws
And it handed me my heart
I felt the blood pouring
from the life of me
Dripping down to soak the
ground
It felt heavy in my hands
And the creature asked me
Would you do it again?
Every mistake
Every tragedy
Every grief filled moment
of it
Could you bear the
weight of it again?
And I lifted my heavy heart
to my lips
Sunk my teeth into the
bitterness
The brokenness
Letting the sting of me coat

my tongue
Yet I did not flinch away
My sorrow overtaking me
with every mouthful
I looked back at the
creature
And I knew myself

And as I spoke the creature
spoke
And I saw myself
Broken
Naked
Bestial
And with blood stained lips
We spoke our answer
Yes.

Made in the USA
Monee, IL
07 July 2026